I0086878

三期盼十

Three Going On Ten

by Yau Ming Ng-Thompson

吴友明/ 著

This book belongs to / 这本书属于：

For Ian and Sean
献给延汉和蒜

版权所有 不准翻印

Copyright © 2018 by Yau Ming Ng. All rights reserved. No part of this publication may be reproduced, stored in a retrieval system, or transmitted in any form or by any means, including photocopying, recording, or other electronic or mechanical methods, without prior written permission of the publisher.

ISBN-13: 978-0692108468

ISBN-10: 0692108467

三期盼十

Three Going On Ten

Yau Ming Ng-Thompson
illustrated by Anna I.

吴友明/ 著
安娜/ 图

It was a nice spring afternoon.
在一个美好的春天下午。

Ian and his daddy were outside trimming bushes in their front yard.
延汉和他的爸爸在屋子前修剪着灌木丛。

Later, Ian ran into the house...
稍后，<u>延汉</u>跑进屋里......

and said, "Mommy,
I want to eat."
说："妈妈，
我想要吃一点东西。"

"Why?" Mommy asked.
"为什么？" 妈妈问。

"I want to be bigger,"
replied Ian.
"我要快点长大，"
延汉回答。

"Why? You just ate lunch not too long ago," said Mommy. "为什么呢？你刚刚才吃过了午卢。"妈妈说。

"Daddy said when I turn ten, I can help with the cutting."
"爸爸说，当我十岁时，我就可以帮他修剪灌木。"

If I eat food, I will get bigger and turn ten.
如果我吃东西，我就会快高长大变成十岁了。

After eating five animal crackers...
当延汉吃完五片动物饼干之后……

Ian went outside where his daddy
was cutting back bushes with a
pair of hedge shears.

延汉出去找爸爸，而
他的爸爸正在用一把
绿篱剪修剪着灌木。

"Daddy, I am bigger. I turned ten,"
Ian said, seriously.
延汉认真的说："爸爸，我长大了。
我已经十岁了。"

"No, you are still three," said Daddy.
"不，你还是三岁。"爸爸说。

His daddy gave him a small pair of pliers instead.

他的爸爸只是给他一把小小的钳子。

Ian held the pliers unwillingly.
延汉不情愿地拿着那把小钳子。

He tried to cut and pull the bushes without success.
他试图修剪灌木，但不成功。

He wanted to use the big hedge shears like his daddy but was not allowed because it was too dangerous.

他想要像爸爸那样使用那把绿篱剪，但是因为太危险而不被允许。

About twenty minutes later, Ian went back into the house and told his mommy that he wanted to eat something else.

大约二十分钟后，延汉回去家里，告诉妈妈他想吃别的东西。

"What do you want to eat?"
asked Mommy.
"你想吃什么？"妈妈问。

Ian pulled his little step stool to the pantry and told his mommy that he wanted to eat jelly beans.

Cornflakes

Peanut Butter

Strawberry Strawberry Strawberry

POTATO

延汉把小凳子拉到厨房的食品储藏室，告诉妈妈他想吃软糖。

Mommy told him jelly beans wouldn't make him bigger and redirected him to the counter.
妈妈告诉他，软糖不会让他快高长大，然后带他走向柜台。

She told him that sweet potatoes would make him healthy and strong.
她告诉他，红薯会使他健康强壮。

Ian ate some sweet potatoes.
延汉吃了一些红薯。

After eating he went outside, rubbing his tummy and said, "Daddy, I turned ten. I am bigger now. Look at my muscles."

吃完后，他走出屋外，揉着肚子说："爸爸，我十岁了。我长大了，看看我的肌肉。"

Daddy said, "Ian, you will be bigger one day, and I hope you will still want to help Daddy when you turn ten."

爸爸说："延汉，有一天你将会长大，我希望当你十岁的时候还会乐意的帮忙爸爸。"

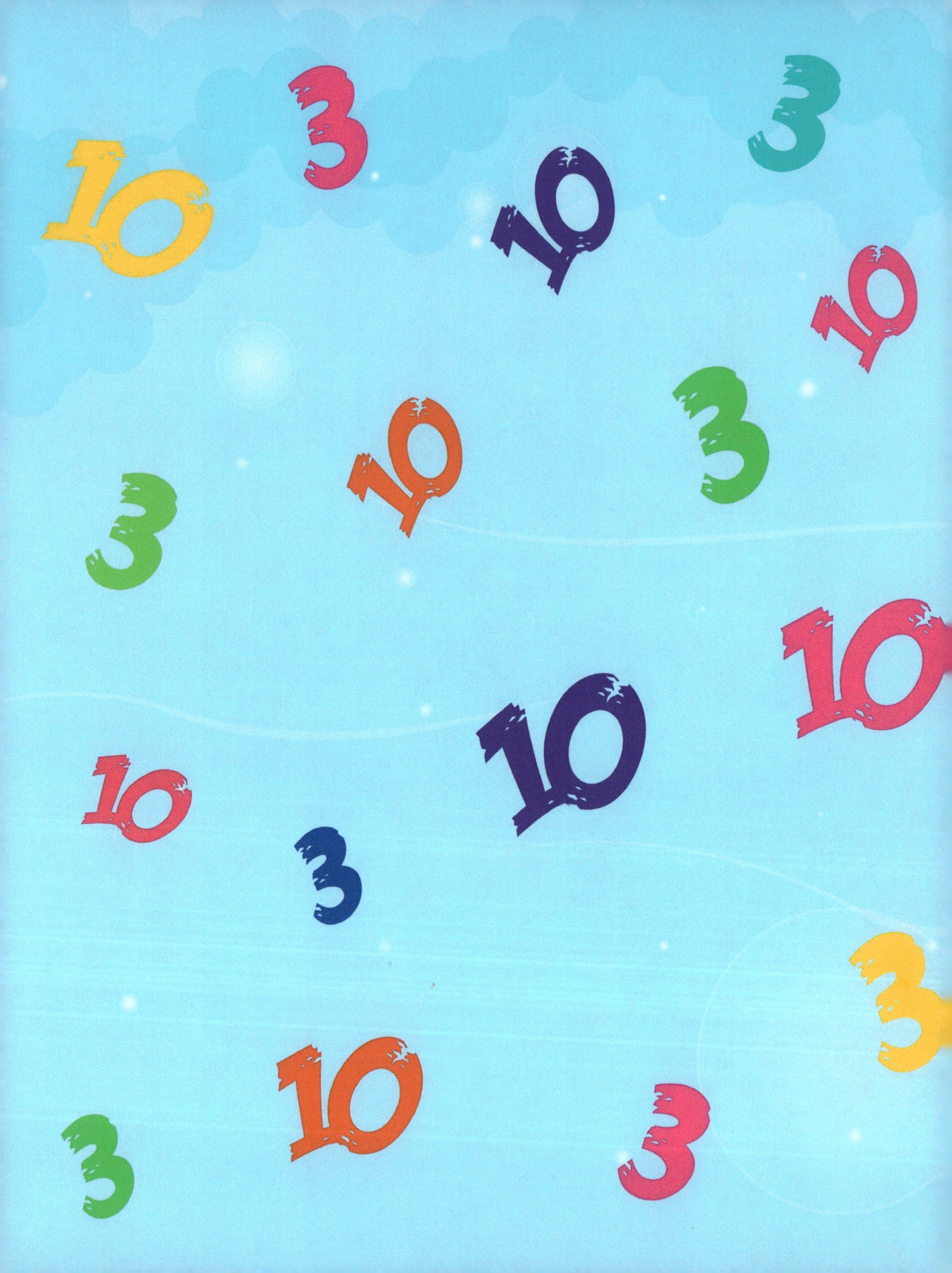

3 3
10 10 10
3
10
3
10
10 10
10
3
10 3
3 3

Thank you for reading my first children's book! I love to write, and writing is my passion! While I was a teenager, I wrote feature stories in Chinese for newspapers in Asia. During college in the United States, I was a staff columnist; I wrote English stories and articles for my college newspaper. I also received an award in a writing contest. As an author and a Registered Dietitian Nutritionist, I also wrote many educational nutrition articles for a hospital newsletter. However, writing for children is new to me. I would love to hear your feedback. Please leave a helpful review on Amazon with your thoughts about this book.
Thank you, Yau Ming Ng-Thompson

谢谢您阅读我的第一本儿童读物！我很喜欢写作，写作是我生活上的动力！在中学时期，我时常写稿给当地的报馆。后来在美国上大学的时候，我曾是一名专栏作者；为校园的报章撰写英文故事和文章。我还在写作比赛中获得了奖项。身为一名作家和营养师，我也曾为医院的时事传报撰写了许多富有教育性的营养学文章。至于撰写儿童故事可是我的新体验哦。我很想听听您的意见。请于亚马逊网站写下您对这本书的感言。在此我也趁这个机会来谢谢简宝苹帮我译校这本书。
谢谢您的支持！
吴友明

www.ingramcontent.com/pod-product-compliance
Lightning Source LLC
Chambersburg PA
CBHW041238040426

42445CB00004B/76